Harvest Mouse

By Ruth Owen

Educational Consultant:
Dee Reid

Tips for Reading with Your Child

- Set aside at least 10 to 15 minutes each day for reading.

- Find a quiet place to sit with no distractions. Turn off the TV, music and screens.

- Encourage your child to hold the book and turn the pages.

- Before reading begins, look at the pictures together and talk about what you see.

- If the reader gets stuck on a word, try reading to the end of the sentence. Often by reading the word in context, he or she will be able to figure out the unknown word. Looking at the pictures can help, too.

- Words shown in **bold** are explained in the glossary on pages 22–23.

Above all enjoy the time together and make reading fun!

Book Band Orange

**For more information about harvest mice go to:
www.rubytuesdaybooks.com/wildlifewatchers**

What do you know about harvest mice?

A harvest mouse has ...

- A long, thin, bendy tail
- A thick, bushy tail
- A short, stubby tail

How much does a harvest mouse weigh?

- The same as an orange
- The same as a 20 pence coin
- The same as a kitten

How does a harvest mouse build a nest?

- It digs a hole in the ground.
- It weaves together strips of grass.
- It builds a nest from twigs and mud.

How big is a baby harvest mouse?

- As big as your head
- As big as your fist
- As big as your thumbnail

Now read this book and find the answers.

It's a warm day in July.

A tiny **harvest** mouse is eating breakfast in a **wheat** field.

She holds onto a stalk of wheat with her back feet and long, bendy tail.

She is eating a wheat seed that she holds in her front feet.

wheat stalk

What other foods does the
hungry harvest mouse eat?

Crunch!

She catches and eats
a grasshopper.

Next, she eats some juicy blackberries.
She needs lots of energy because
today she is building a **nest**.

First, the harvest mouse chooses a place to build her nest.

These poppy stems are too bendy.

These thick grass stems are just right.

She can climb up plant stems because she is very light.

She only weighs as much as a 20 pence coin!

To build her nest the mouse tears grass into thin strips with her teeth.

strips of grass

She **weaves** the strips of grass together to make a round nest.

She fixes the nest to some thick grass stems.

nest

The nest is the same size
as a tennis ball.

The next day, the harvest mouse gives birth to five babies inside her nest.

The babies have no fur and they cannot see.

The baby mice drink milk from their mother's body.

The mother mouse licks the babies to keep them clean.

The baby harvest mice are only as big as your thumbnail.

After five days, they have grown some brown fur.

Their eyes are forming, too.

When the babies go to the toilet, the mother mouse eats their poo.

This helps to keep the nest clean.

five-day-old mouse

The mother mouse and her babies are in danger!

weasel

A **weasel** has come to live close to their nest in the wheat field.

Weasels hunt for mice and other small animals.

The mother mouse must protect her babies from the hungry weasel.

She builds a new nest in a different part of the field.

Then one by one she carries her babies to their new, safe home.

Every day, the mother mouse leaves the nest to find food.

She eats lots of seeds, berries and **insects**.

When she gets home, she feeds the babies by sicking up food into their mouths.

Once the babies are 12 days old,
they leave the nest.

They explore
and practise
climbing up
plant stems.

Sometimes, the tiny brothers and sisters hold onto each other with their tails.

This helps them to balance on plant stems.

At two weeks old, the baby mice no longer live with their mother.

Now they can find their own food and take care of themselves.

Once they are six weeks old, they will be ready to have babies of their own!

Glossary

harvest
To cut down or gather fruit, vegetables or crops such as wheat and barley.

insect
A small animal with six legs and a body in three parts. An insect does not have bones. Instead it has a hard outer shell called an exoskeleton.

nest
An animal's home that it builds from materials such as twigs, grass, leaves or mud.

weasel
An animal with a long, thin, furry body. Weasels hunt and eat mice and other small animals.

weave
To join long threads of string, wool or another material together by lacing the threads under and over each other.

wheat
A type of grass plant that is grown for food. The seeds of wheat plants are made into flour for baking bread, biscuits and cakes.

Harvest Mouse
Quiz

1 What foods did the harvest mouse eat?

2 How big is the harvest mouse's nest?

3 What things does the harvest mouse do to take care of her babies?

4 How is the newborn mouse on page 12 similar to the mother mouse? How is it different?

5 Which fact about harvest mice did you like best? Why?